Wonderfully Made

Kaitlyn Derosiers and Megan McBryde

This book is dedicated to our parents, Ken and Kathy.
We are blessed by your courage, your love, and your wisdom.
To Pop-Pop, Ga and Grandma Catherine,
thank you for always being the light and joy in our lives.

Wonderfully Made

This is Katie and Tessa. Katie and Tessa are sisters.
They have beautiful curly hair
and skin the color of caramel.

Kaite and Tessa love running on the playground, going to school and playing fetch with their dog, Cleo.

But most of all, Katie and Tessa love their family.

Katie and Tessa's mom has short, wavy brown hair
and striking blue eyes. Her skin is as sweet
as a light apricot on a warm spring day.

Their dad has short black hair and warm brown eyes.
His skin is as comforting as hot chocolate
on a cold snowy day.

Katie has her dad's nose and her mom's smile.
Tessa has her mom's hands and her dad's ears.
They are wonderfully made.

Over the weekend, Katie and Tessa visit with their Grandparents.
PopPop teaches Katie and Tessa
how to make crepes.

Crepes can be sweet with fruit or chocolate.
But crepes can also be made with meat, cheese, or eggs.
You can eat crepes for breakfast, lunch, and dinner too!

At grandma Catherine's, Dad shows them the picture of their great grandma and tells them stories about growing up on the sharecroppers farm down south.

Aunts and uncles smile
as they share stories and pictures
of the old church and schoolhouse.

On Monday morning, Katie and Tessa's mom and dad drop them off at school. There are a lot of students at their school and most of them don't look like Katie and Tessa.
Sometimes, Katie and Tessa are asked questions that can be hard to answer.

Sometimes, the kids at school ask Katie and Tessa questions about how they look or about their family. These questions can be difficult to answer because, to Katie and Tessa, their family is just their family!

These kinds of questions really make Katie and Tessa think and they are curious about why some people see them and their family as "different".

One afternoon, Katie's class goes on a field trip
to their town's library.
Katie's mom goes with the class as a parent chaperone.

"Is that your mom?" Jeremiah asks.
"She doesn't look like you."
Jeremiah sounded confused,
like he couldn't figure out or see
how Katie and her mom fit together.

While Katie's class
was visiting the library,
Tessa's class did a "My Family Tree"
project at school.
Everyone brought in different pictures of their families.

It was fun to see all the pictures of her classmate's families. However, Tessa definitely noticed that her family pictures looked different than most everyone else's.

Katie and Tessa think of so many wonderful memories and it makes them happy. They love all the great things about their family.
They are wonderfully made.

Katie does not want people to be confused about who they are.
Katie knows that people
ask questions to help them understand.
She wants to help people learn.

With excitement, Katie says, "Yes, that's my mom, we have the same smile! Not all family members look exactly the same." Katie is wonderfully made.

Tessa wants people to know that they love their family and are proud to be part of it.

Tessa proudly shares her family tree. She explains to the class that family members don't always look exactly alike but they love each other just the same.

Tessa is excited to point out how she has her mother's hands and her father's ears.

Tessa is wonderfully made.

Katie and Tessa know that their family is filled with love and rich history.
So now when Katie and Tessa are asked hard questions, they remember all the wonderful things that make them unique. They can speak confidently and proudly about who they are.

They know they are **Wonderfully Made.**

We are all
Wonderfully Made.

"I will praise You, for I am fearfully
and wonderfully made;
Marvelous are Your works,
And that my soul knows very well."
-Psalm 139:14

Made in the USA
Coppell, TX
01 April 2021

52849392R00026